The Recipe list

ANDREW JACKSON

7th President (March 4, 1829 – March 4, 1837)
Vice President: John C. Calhoun (1829–1832)
None (1832–1833)
Martin Van Buren (1833–1837)

"Take time to deliberate; but when the time for action arrives, stop thinking and go in."

DID YOU KNOW?

Andrew Jackson loved cheese. As a gift, a dairy farmer sent the president a 1,400-pound cheese wheel covered in patriotic inscriptions. Before Jackson left office, he invited 10,000 guests to sample the cheese. Maybe that's why he was called the "People's President."

The HANGRY DEMOCRAT Cookbook

JZ BOOKS

ISBN: 9781730925757

DID YOU KNOW?

U.S. presidents have to pay for their own groceries!

Cauliflower Mac 'n' Cheese

INGREDIENTS

1 head of cauliflower
1/4 teaspoon of garlic powder
1/2 teaspoon of paprika
2 ounces of cream cheese
1 cup of shredded cheddar cheese
2 tablespoons of grated parmesan cheese
Parsley
Salt and pepper to taste

DIRECTIONS

Cut cauliflower into small florets.
Bring 6 cups of water to a boil in a small pot. Add cauliflower and boil until tender, about 5 minutes. Drain, and return cauliflower to the pot. Over low heat, add garlic powder, paprika, cream cheese, cheddar cheese, parmesan, salt and pepper. Stir frequently, and continue cooking until all cheese is melted and spread evenly over cauliflower. Serve immediately. Serves 2-4.

Salt & Vinegar Popcorn

INGREDIENTS

8 cups of plain popped popcorn
3 tablespoons of butter
3 teaspoons of white vinegar
1 teaspoon of salt
1 teaspoon of dried dill

DIRECTIONS

Melt butter. Blend in vinegar and mix well. Slowly pour over popcorn, mixing the popcorn as you go so no piece gets too saturated. Sprinkle with salt and dried dill, and serve. Serves 4-6.

"Any man worth his **salt** will stick up for what he believes right, but it takes a slightly better man to acknowledge instantly and without reservation that he is in error." ANDREW JACKSON

DID YOU KNOW?

Jacksonian democracy was a 19th century movement in American government led by Jackson. The philosophy supported greater rights for the common man and opposed aristocracy.

MARTIN VAN BUREN

8th President (March 4, 1837 – March 4, 1841)
Vice President: Richard Mentor Johnson

"The government should not be guided by temporary excitement, but by sober second thought."

DID YOU KNOW?

Van Buren's biggest challenge as president was a financial crisis known as the Panic of 1837, which set off a major recession. Van Buren's opponents wanted to recharter a national bank, but Van Buren instead established the Independent Treasury to manage the nation's money supply. Although this decision was criticized at the time, modern economists view his economic policy as a success.

For when you want to be guided by sober thought ...

Ginger Peach Smoothie

INGREDIENTS

2 peaches, chopped
5 ounces of vanilla yogurt
2 teaspoons of chopped ginger
1 tablespoon of honey
1/4 cup of water

DIRECTIONS

Combine all ingredients in blender and mix well. Serves 2.

Ginger is a great remedy for an upset stomach ... just in case you were guided by temporary excitement the night before.

DID YOU KNOW?

Martin Van Buren was the first president born as an American citizen, and not a British subject.

JAMES K. POLK

11th President (March 4, 1845 – March 4, 1849)
Vice President: George M. Dallas

GREAT MOMENT IN HISTORY

In December 1845, Polk signed a resolution annexing Texas, which became the 28th state. The territory of the United States eventually grew by more than one-third during Polk's presidency and, for the first time, became a coast-to-coast nation.

Texas Chili

INGREDIENTS

1 tablespoon of olive oil
1 onion, diced
2 pounds of ground beef
3 tablespoons of chili powder
1 1/2 teaspoon of paprika
1 teaspoon of cumin
1/2 teaspoon of mustard powder
1/4 teaspoon of cayenne pepper
1/2 teaspoon of dried oregano
1/2 teaspoon of allspice
2 cloves of garlic, chopped
1/2 cup of red wine
1 28-ounce can crushed tomatoes
1/4 cube of beef bouillon
Salt and pepper to taste
Chopped scallions, shredded cheddar cheese and sour cream for garnish

DIRECTIONS

In large skillet, heat olive oil over medium heat. Add onion and cook until softened, about 5 minutes. Add ground beef, chili powder, paprika, cumin, mustard powder, cayenne pepper, oregano, allspice, garlic, salt and pepper. Cook beef, stirring occasionally, until well-browned, about 6-8 minutes.

Add crushed tomatoes, red wine and beef bouillon, and stir to combine. Cover and reduce heat to low. Cook for 2 hours. Serve with scallions, cheddar cheese and sour cream if desired. Serves 4-6.

"No president who performs his duties faithfully and conscientiously can have any leisure."

Not enough leisure in your life? Eat more salmon! Salmon is packed with omega-3 fatty acids, which can reduce anxiety and improve your ability to deal with stress.

Salmon Burgers

INGREDIENTS

1 1/4 pounds of salmon fillet, skin and bones removed
2 tablespoons of dijon mustard
1 tablespoon of mayonnaise
1 tablespoon of lemon juice
2 scallions, chopped
Pinch of cayenne pepper
Salt and pepper to taste
1 cup plus 2 tablespoons of panko bread crumbs
3 tablespoons of olive oil

For the tarter sauce:
1 cup of mayonnaise
1 cup of finely chopped dill pickles
1 tablespoon of dried dill
1 teaspoon of lemon juice
1 teaspoon of sugar
1/4 teaspoon of black pepper

DIRECTIONS

Combine all ingredients for tarter sauce and refrigerate.

Cut half the salmon into 1/4-inch pieces and place into a large bowl. Roughly cut the rest of salmon and place in blender with the mustard, mayonnaise, lemon juice, cayenne, salt and pepper. Blend into a paste. Transfer mixture to bowl with chopped salmon. Add scallion and 2 tablespoons of bread crumbs, and mix.

Divide salmon mixture into 4 parts, and form into patties. Cover with plastic wrap and refrigerate for at least 30 minutes.

Remove patties from fridge, and brush with olive oil. Press remaining 1 cup of Panko crumbs into each side of all patties.

Heat 2 tablespoons of olive oil in skillet over medium heat. When hot, place salmon patties in skillet, and cook about 3-4 minutes until brown. Flip, and cook an additional 3-4 minutes until cooked through.

Drain on paper towel. Serve with tarter sauce, either alone or on buns. Serves 4.

Kiwi Cocktail

INGREDIENTS

3 kiwi, peeled and sliced
2 teaspoons of lime juice
8 mint leaves
5 ounces of seltzer
5 ounces of rum

INGREDIENTS

Combine all ingredients in blender and blend until smooth. Serve over ice. Serves 4.

"There is nothing left to do but get drunk."

FRANKLIN PIERCE, WHEN LEAVING OFFICE

FRANKLIN PIERCE

14th President (March 4, 1853 – March 4, 1857)
Vice President: William R. King (1853)
None (1853–1857)

GREAT MOMENT IN HISTORY:

On June 24, 1853, Pierce signed a treaty to purchase a region of land from Mexico that later became southern portions of Arizona and New Mexico.

JAMES BUCHANAN

15th President (March 4, 1857 – March 4, 1861)
Vice President: John C. Breckinridge

"I like the **noise** of democracy."

Crunchy Cabbage Salad

Cabbage was one of James Buchanan's favorite vegetables!

INGREDIENTS

3 cups of red cabbage, shredded
1 cup of carrots, grated
1 cup of bean sprouts
1/2 cup of green onions, chopped
8 ounces of shelled edamame
1/2 cup of peanuts
1 package of ramen noodles

For the dressing:
1/2 cup of sesame oil
1/4 cup of honey
1/4 cup of apple cider vinegar
2 tablespoons of soy sauce
1 teaspoon of ginger, finely grated

DIRECTIONS

Mix ingredients for dressing and set aside. Combine cabbage, carrots, bean sprouts, green onions, edamame and peanuts in a large bowl and mix well. Break raw ramen noodles into small pieces and toss with salad. Cover with dressing and serve immediately. Serves 4.

ANDREW JOHNSON

17th President (April 15, 1865 - March 4, 1869)
Vice President: None

DID YOU KNOW?

Johnson became president after Abraham Lincoln died. Johnson was a member of the Democratic Party before the Civil War, and had been Lincoln's 1864 running mate on the National Union ticket.

GROVER CLEVELAND

22nd President (March 4, 1885 – March 4, 1889)
Vice President: Thomas A. Hendricks (1885)
None (1885–1889)

24th President (March 4, 1893 – March 4, 1897)
Vice President: Adlai Stevenson I

"What is the use of being elected or re-elected, unless you stand for something?"

GREAT MOMENT IN HISTORY

Cleveland's election in 1884 broke a losing streak for Democrats of six consecutive elections, the longest streak for a major political party in the United States. Cleveland was one of only two Democrats to be elected during a period of Republican domination from 1861 to 1933. Cleveland is also the only U.S. president to serve nonconsecutive terms.

Beer-Braised Short Ribs

INGREDIENTS

2 pounds of beef short ribs
1 tablespoon of olive oil
1 red onion, chopped
2 celery stalks, chopped
2 carrots, sliced
4 garlic cloves, chopped
2 tablespoons of tomato paste
1 12-ounce bottle of lager beer
2 tablespoons of Worcestershire sauce
1 1/2 cups of beef broth
1 1/2 tablespoons of flour
Salt and pepper to taste

DIRECTIONS

Season ribs with salt and pepper. Heat olive oil in a cast iron skillet over medium heat. Add ribs to pan, and fry about 3 minutes on each side until brown. Remove ribs from pan and set aside.

Add onion, celery and carrots to pan and sauté for 5 minutes. Stir in garlic and tomato paste, and sauté an additional 2 minutes. Add beer, Worcestershire sauce, and beef broth to pan, and mix well.

Return ribs to pan, turning to coat with sauce. Cover and bake at 350 degrees for 3 hours, until ribs are tender.

Transfer ribs to serving platter. Skim fat from sauce remaining in skillet. Over medium heat, slowly add flour to skillet and mix well. Bring to a boil, and boil for 1 minute. Pour over ribs, and serve. Serves 2-4. Tip: Works well with egg noodles or mashed potatoes.

DID YOU KNOW?

Cleveland was the second-heaviest president at 250 pounds, in part because of his love of beer drinking. Born Stephen Grover Cleveland, his nicknames were "Big Steve" and "Uncle Jumbo."

WOODROW WILSON

28th President (March 4, 1913 – March 4, 1921)
Vice President: Thomas R. Marshall

"Tell me what is right, and I will fight for it."

GREAT MOMENT IN HISTORY

Wilson's approval was critical in the eventual passing of the 19th Amendment, which prohibits any U.S. citizen from being denied the right to vote on the basis of gender. After realizing the important contributions of women during World War I, Wilson publicly endorsed before Congress a woman's right to vote, despite opposition in his own party. Another year would pass before the 19th Amendment was ratified, but Wilson's support was a turning point for women's rights.

Girl Power Pasta

INGREDIENTS

1 large beet
8 ounces of ricotta cheese
2 tablespoons of lemon juice
2 tablespoons of olive oil
Salt to taste
8 ounces of cooked pasta
1/4 cup of fresh cilantro, chopped
4 ounces of fresh parmesan, grated

DIRECTIONS

Roughly chop beet into pieces. Transfer to pot and cover with water. Bring water to a boil over medium heat, then reduce to low heat and simmer until beets are soft, about 45 minutes. Drain, and rinse with cold water.

Transfer beets to blender, and combine with ricotta cheese, lemon juice, olive oil and salt. Blend well. Return beet sauce to pot and reheat.

Serve over cooked pasta, topped with cilantro and parmesan cheese. Serves 4.

Pulled Pork Sliders

INGREDIENTS

1 boneless pork shoulder, about 3 pounds
2 tablespoons of brown sugar
1 tablespoon of paprika
1 teaspoon of cumin
1 tablespoon of salt
1 teaspoon of black pepper
1 onion, chopped
1/2 cup of chicken broth
2 tablespoons of balsamic vinegar
Slider buns

For the barbecue sauce:

1 cup of ketchup
2 tablespoons of brown sugar
1 tablespoon of soy sauce
1 tablespoon of Worcestershire sauce
2 tablespoons of apple cider vinegar
1/8 teaspoon of red pepper flakes
1 clove of garlic, minced

DIRECTIONS

In a small bowl, combine brown sugar, paprika, cumin, salt and black pepper. Massage into pork.

Add onions and chicken broth to slow cooker, and place pork on top. Cook on low heat for 8 hours. In the meantime, combine ingredients for barbecue sauce in a small pan. Simmer over low heat for 15 minutes. Set aside and cool.

Remove meat from slow cooker. Cut the pork into slices, trimming the fat. Strain liquid remaining in the slow cooker to remove fat and onions. Return liquid to slow cooker along with pork slices. Add half of the barbecue sauce, and cook for an additional 1 hour on low heat.

Drain excess liquid, shred pork with fork, and top with remaining barbecue sauce. Serve on slider buns.

GREAT MOMENT IN HISTORY

In 1916, the U.S. economy was threatened by a railroad worker strike. Wilson settled the issue by proposing a maximum eight-hour work day, with additional pay for overtime. The strike was cancelled, and Wilson was praised for avoiding an economic disaster.

Thanks to Wilson, quittin' time is never too far away! Host your own happy hour with these delicious appetizers.

Baked Corn Dip

INGREDIENTS

4 cups of corn
1 red pepper, diced
1 green pepper, diced
2 jalapeño peppers, diced and seeds removed
2 tablespoons of butter
1 teaspoon of garlic powder
1/2 teaspoon of paprika
1/2 teaspoon of cumin
4 ounces of cream cheese
2 cups of grated cheddar cheese
Salt and pepper to taste
Chopped cilantro for garnish

DIRECTIONS

Heat butter in skillet over medium heat. Add all peppers, garlic powder, paprika, cumin, salt and pepper, and sauté for 3-5 minutes until peppers are soft. Tip: Include some jalapeño seeds for a spicier dip. Turn heat to low, add cream cheese, and stir until well-blended.

Transfer to a baking dish. Add corn and half of the cheddar cheese, and mix well. Top with remaining cheddar. Bake at 350 degrees for 20 minutes. You may choose to broil for the last few minutes until the cheese on top is golden brown. Sprinkle with chopped cilantro, and serve with tortilla chips.

DID YOU KNOW?

Wilson signed into law the Federal Reserve Act in 1913. This established the Federal Reserve System, the central banking system of the United States.

In 1914, Wilson established the Federal Trade Commission to regulate questionable business practices.

FRANKLIN D. ROOSEVELT

32nd President (March 4, 1933 – April 12, 1945)
Vice President: John N. Garner (1933–1941)
Henry A. Wallace (1941–1945)
Harry S. Truman (1945)

"Take a method and try it. If it fails, admit it frankly, and try another. But by all means, try something."

DID YOU KNOW?

FDR was the longest-serving U.S. president, winning four elections. The two-term limit wasn't established until after his presidency.

GREAT MOMENT IN HISTORY

Under FDR's watch, the 21st Amendment to the Constitution was passed and ratified in 1933, ending national Prohibition. Bottoms up!

DID YOU KNOW?

FDR was the first president to travel by airplane on official U.S. business. On the flight home, he celebrated his 61st birthday in the air, enjoying caviar, olives, celery, pickles, turkey, green peas, cake and champagne.

Champagne Punch

INGREDIENTS

1 bottle of champagne
1 cup of pineapple juice
1 cup of orange juice
1 orange, sliced
1 lime, sliced
1/2 cup of sliced strawberries

DIRECTIONS

Combine champagne, pineapple juice and orange juice in a large bowl. Float fruit slices on top. Serves 6.

RED, WHITE & BLUE

"I pledge you, I pledge myself, to a new deal for the American people."

FDR is famous for the "New Deal", a series of domestic programs instituted during the Great Depression to restore prosperity to Americans. Among the highlights:

The Civilian Conservation Corps was a work relief program that provided jobs for many Americans.

The Federal Housing Administration was designed to regulate mortgages and housing conditions.

The Public Works Administration spent more than $6 billion on large-scale construction.

The Federal Emergency Relief Administration gave states funds to operate relief programs.

The Agricultural Adjustment Administration boosted agricultural prices by reducing surpluses.

Tomato Soup with Shrimp & Feta Cheese

INGREDIENTS

2 tablespoons of butter
1 onion, chopped
2 carrots, chopped
2 cloves of garlic, chopped
1 15-ounce can of white beans, drained and rinsed
8 medium tomatoes, peeled and chopped
3 cups of chicken broth
1 bay leaf
1 teaspoon of dried rosemary
1/2 teaspoon of red pepper flakes
1 pound of shrimp, peeled
5 ounces of feta cheese
Salt and pepper to taste

DIRECTIONS

In a large pot, melt butter over medium heat. Add onion, carrot and garlic, and cook until vegetables are tender, about 5 minutes. Add tomatoes, beans, chicken broth, bay leaf, rosemary and red pepper flakes to pot. Bring to a boil, then reduce heat and simmer for 30 minutes covered. Remove bay leaf and puree soup in a blender in batches. Return soup to pot. Add salt, pepper, shrimp and goat cheese. Cook over medium heat until shrimp are no longer opaque, about 5-8 minutes. Serves 4-8.

Horseradish Mashed Potatoes

INGREDIENTS

5 potatoes, peeled and quartered
2 tablespoons of butter
1/2 cup of sour cream
1 1/2 tablespoons of horseradish
Salt and pepper to taste
Parsley for garnish

DIRECTIONS

Bring a large pot of salted water to a boil. Add potatoes and cook until tender, about 15 minutes. Return potatoes to pot and mash. Add butter and mix until melted. Add sour cream, horseradish, salt and pepper, and blend well. Serve with parsley sprinkled on top. Serves 4.

Blue State Italian Ice

INGREDIENTS

1 cup of boiling water
2 cups of lemon-lime soda
1 3-ounce package of blue gelatin powder

DIRECTIONS

Dissolve gelatin in cup of boiling water. Stir in soda pop. Freeze at least four hours. Use an ice cream scoop to serve. Serves 4-6.

"The only thing we have to fear is fear itself. Nameless, unreasoning, unjustified terror, which paralyzes needed efforts to convert retreat into advance."

DID YOU KNOW?

The U.S. social security system was created during Roosevelt's presidency. He also established the first national minimum wage.

GREAT MOMENT IN HISTORY

Roosevelt delivered his famous "Infamy Speech" on Dec. 8, 1941, one day after Japan's attack on the U.S. naval base at Pearl Harbor. He described the event as "a date which will live in infamy," and his speech went down as one of the most famous in U.S. history. Within one hour, Congress passed a formal declaration of war against Japan and officially brought the United States into World War II.

French Onion Grilled Cheese

INGREDIENTS

3 large onions, sliced
2 tablespoons of olive oil
1/4 teaspoon of sugar
1 tablespoon of sherry
1 tablespoon of beef broth
1/4 teaspoon of dried thyme
1 loaf of French bread
16 ounces of Swiss cheese
2-3 tablespoons of butter

DIRECTIONS

Heat olive oil in skillet over medium heat. Add sliced onions and reduce heat to low. After cooking a few minutes, sprinkle sugar on top. Continue cooking onions for about 45 minutes, stirring occasionally until they begin to caramelize. (Note: If onions begin to burn, reduce heat.)

When onions are caramelized, add sherry, beef broth and thyme. Cook onions a few minutes longer, until liquid has evaporated. Set onions aside.

Slice French bread into pieces about 1/2-inch thick. Butter one side of each piece. Make sandwiches with cheese and onions, leaving the buttered side of bread slices on the outside.

Fry sandwiches in a skillet over medium heat, about 3-4 minutes on each side, until the bread begins to brown and the cheese is melted. Makes about 6 small sandwiches.

FDR's favorite food was grilled cheese sandwiches!

HARRY TRUMAN

33rd President (April 12, 1945 – Jan. 20, 1953)
Vice President: None (1945–1949)
Alben W. Barkley (1949–1953)

DID YOU KNOW?

Truman liked his steak well done. He believed that "only coyotes and predatory animals eat raw beef."

Enjoy your steak well done like Truman!

Slow Cooker Pepper Steak

INGREDIENTS

1 1/2 pounds of round steak, cut into thin strips
1 green pepper, sliced
1 red pepper, sliced
1 onion, sliced
1 1/2 cups of beef stock
3 tablespoons of soy sauce
1/4 teaspoon of ground ginger
1/4 teaspoon of garlic powder
2 teaspoons of brown sugar
1 tablespoon of cornstarch
Salt and pepper to taste

DIRECTIONS

Place the beef, peppers and onions in the slow cooker. Add soy sauce, ginger, garlic powder, brown sugar, salt and pepper and mix well. Pour beef stock on top and mix. Cook on low for 4 hours.

Mix cornstarch with 1/4 cup of cold water. Add to slow cooker, turn heat to high, and continue cooking for 2 hours. Optional: Serve with sesame seeds over white rice. Serves 4-6.

Meatless Meatloaf

INGREDIENTS

2 cups of cooked lentils
1 small onion, diced
1 carrot, chopped
2 celery stalks, diced
1/2 cup of red pepper, diced
6 mushrooms, chopped
1 clove of garlic, minced
1 tablespoon of olive oil
2 tablespoons of tomato paste
1 tablespoon of barbecue sauce
1 egg
1/2 cup of oats
1/2 cup of bread crumbs

For the glaze:
1/2 cup of ketchup
1 teaspoon of dijon mustard
1 teaspoon of apple cider vinegar
Sprinkle of sugar

DIRECTIONS

Heat olive oil in large skillet over medium heat. Sauté onion, carrots, celery, red pepper, and mushrooms until softened, 3-5 minutes. Add garlic and sauté 1 minute.

In a blender, combine cooked lentils, vegetables from skillet, tomato paste, barbecue sauce, egg, oats and bread crumbs and blend just enough to mix ingredients. Tip: For a chunkier loaf, set aside half of the veggies, and add after blending is finished.

In a separate bowl, combine ketchup, mustard and apple cider vinegar and set aside.

Cover a baking sheet with parchment paper. Spoon mixture onto paper, and form into a rectangular meatloaf shape, about 2 inches deep. Bake at 350 degrees for 35 minutes. Remove from the oven and spread glaze evenly on top. Sprinkle loaf with sugar and return to over for 10 minutes. Let loaf cool for 10 minutes before serving. Serves 4.

"Always be sincere, even if you don't mean it."

HARRY TRUMAN

This "meatloaf" doesn't mean it!

“If you can’t stand the heat, get out of the kitchen.”

HARRY TRUMAN

Can’t stand the heat? These recipes require no cooking!

Cucumber & Avocado Soup

INGREDIENTS

2 cucumbers, peeled and chopped
1 avocado
1 serrano pepper, chopped
1/4 cup of chopped red onion
1/2 cup of plain Greek yogurt
1 clove of garlic, chopped
1 tablespoon of fresh dill
1/4 teaspoon of salt
1/4 cup of water
Chopped scallions for garnish

DIRECTIONS

Combine all ingredients in blender and blend until smooth. Chill for 1 hour, and serve garnished with chopped scallions. Serves 2-4.

GREAT MOMENT IN HISTORY

In 1951, Truman made the first live nationwide broadcast.

Healthy Tuna Wraps

INGREDIENTS

2 cans of tuna, drained
1/2 cup of chopped cucumber
1/2 cup of chopped tomato
1/2 cup of chopped red onion
1 celery stalk, chopped
10 fresh basil leaves, chopped
1/2 cup of balsamic vinegar dressing
1 tablespoon of garlic, minced
Salt to taste
4 lettuce leaves

DIRECTIONS

Combine all ingredients besides lettuce and mix well. Serve tuna in lettuce leaves. Serves 4.

JOHN F. KENNEDY

35th President (Jan. 20, 1961 – Nov. 22, 1963)
Vice President: Lyndon B. Johnson

"Things do not happen. Things are made to happen."

DID YOU KNOW?

Kennedy was the only president to earn a Purple Heart, awarded for his service in the Pacific during World War II.

One of Kennedy's favorite dishes was this fish chowder!

DID YOU KNOW?

JFK established the Peace Corps in 1961.

Fish Chowder

INGREDIENTS

2 pounds of haddock
2 ounces of salt pork, diced
(may substitute 8 slices of bacon)
2 onions, sliced
4 potatoes, diced
1 cup of celery, chopped
1 bay leaf
1 teaspoon of salt
Pepper to taste
1 quart of milk
2 tablespoons of butter

DIRECTIONS

Place the haddock in a large pot with 2 cups water. Simmer for 15 minutes. Drain, reserving the broth. Remove bones from fish and set aside.

Sauté the salt pork (or fry the bacon strips) in the pot until crisp. Remove pork and set aside. In remaining fat, sauté the onions until golden brown, about 5 minutes. Add fish, potatoes, celery, bay leaf, salt and pepper.

Add reserved fish broth, plus extra water if necessary to make 3 total cups of liquid. Simmer for 30 minutes. Add milk and butter, and simmer for 5 more minutes. Serve the chowder sprinkled with diced pork or crumbled bacon. Serves 4-8.

> *"There are risks and costs to action. But they are far less than the long-range risks of comfortable inaction."*
>
> JOHN F. KENNEDY

GREAT MOMENT IN HISTORY

The Cuban Missile Crisis, a tense 13-day confrontation between the United States and the Soviet Union, came to a peaceful end thanks to a compromise proposed by Kennedy. Cuban leader Fidel Castro made an alliance with the Soviets, who began to install nuclear missiles in Cuba. An American spy plane captured photographs of the missile installations, and Kennedy decided to place Cuba under quarantine. The intense standoff could have led to war, but Kennedy instead convinced the Soviet Union to dismantle its weapons in Cuba, while the United States agreed that they would not invade Cuba without cause.

Breakfast Burrito

INGREDIENTS

4 eggs
1/4 cup of chopped jalapeño
1/4 cup of chopped green pepper
1/4 cup of chopped red pepper
1/4 cup of chopped onion
1/2 cup of chopped tomato
1 clove of garlic, minced
1/4 teaspoon of chili powder
1/8 teaspoon of cumin
1/8 teaspoon of cayenne pepper
1/2 cup of cheddar cheese
2 tortillas
1 tablespoon of olive oil
1 tablespoon of butter
Salt and pepper to taste

DIRECTIONS

Break eggs into bowl and whisk. Heat 1/2 tablespoon of olive oil in skillet. Add eggs to skillet and scramble, stirring frequently until eggs are set. Remove from skillet and set aside in a large bowl.

Heat remaining olive oil in skillet. Add jalapeño, green pepper, red pepper, onion, tomato, garlic, chili powder, cumin and cayenne pepper to pan and cook until vegetables are tender, stirring occasionally, about 5 minutes. Transfer vegetables to bowl with eggs and combine.

Lay a tortilla on flat surface. Spread a 1/4 cup of cheddar cheese in the middle. Spoon half the eggs and vegetables on top. Fold tortilla to create a burrito, wrapping as tightly as possible. Repeat with remaining tortilla and ingredients.

Heat butter in skillet over medium heat. Add burritos to skillet, and pan fry a few minutes on each side, until tortillas begin to brown. Optional: Serve with sour cream and hot sauce. Serves 2.

GREAT MOMENT IN HISTORY

On May 25, 1961, Kennedy delivered a powerful speech that proposed putting a human on the moon by the end of the decade. The speech jump-started NASA's Apollo program, and on July 20, 1969, American astronauts Neil Armstrong and Buzz Aldrin became the first humans to walk on the moon.

Eat like an astronaut: Tortillas work better than bread on space missions because there are fewer crumbs!

Croque Monsieur

INGREDIENTS

2 tablespoons of butter
3 tablespoons of flour
2 cups of hot milk
1 teaspoon of salt
5 cups of grated Gruyère cheese
1/2 cup of grated Parmesan
16 slices of white bread with the crusts removed
Dijon mustard
8 slices of Virginia ham

DIRECTIONS

Melt butter in saucepan over low heat. Add flour, and mix to blend. Add warm milk a little at a time, stirring continuously, until sauce is well-blended and thick. Remove from heat. Add 1/2 cup of Gruyère cheese, parmesan, salt and pepper and mix well. Set aside.

Lay bread slices on a baking sheet. Bake at 400 degrees for 3 minutes. Flip slices, and bake an additional 3 minutes, until toasted.

Brush half the bread slices with dijon mustard. Lay a piece of ham on top. Sprinkle half the remaining shredded Gruyère cheese on top of ham.

Use the remaining 8 bread slices as the sandwich tops. Pour cheese mixture generously on top of sandwiches. Sprinkle remaining shredded Gruyère cheese on top. Return to oven for 5 minutes. Then broil sandwiches for 2-3 minutes, until tops are golden brown. Serves 8.

DID YOU KNOW?

JFK made a serious effort to learn French, and eventually sought help from his daughter Caroline's tutor. But he was never able to grasp the language.

If you can't speak French, you can still cook French!

"And so, my fellow Americans, ask not what your country can do for you - ask what you can do for your country." JOHN F. KENNEDY

GREAT MOMENT IN HISTORY

Kennedy signed into law the Equal Pay Act of 1963 to abolish wage disparity based on sex.

LYNDON B. JOHNSON

36th President (Nov. 22, 1963 – Jan. 20, 1969)
Vice President: None (1963–1965)
Hubert Humphrey (1965–1969)

"Until justice is blind to **color**, *until education is unaware of race, until opportunity is unconcerned with the color of men's skins, emancipation will be a proclamation but not a fact."*

Rainbow Salad

INGREDIENTS

2 cups of fresh spinach leaves
1 cup of grape tomatoes, sliced
1 can of chick peas, rinsed
1 avocado, sliced
1 small mango, sliced
1/4 cup of red onion, thinly sliced
1/2 cucumber, thinly sliced

For the dressing:
Juice of 2 limes
1/4 cup of fresh cilantro
2 cloves of garlic, finely chopped
1 teaspoon of honey
1/4 cup of olive oil
1 tablespoon of jalapeño, finely chopped
Salt and pepper to taste

DIRECTIONS

Combine ingredients for dressing in a bowl and set aside. Combine salad in a separate bowl and toss well. Top with dressing. Serves 4.

GREAT MOMENT IN HISTORY

In 1964, Johnson signed into law the Civil Rights Act, a landmark law that banned discrimination based on race, color, religion, sex or national origin. The Act prohibited discrimination in public places, provided for the integration of schools, and made employment discrimination illegal.

"I want to make a policy statement. I am unabashedly in favor of women."

LYNDON B. JOHNSON

GREAT MOMENT IN HISTORY

The War on Poverty is the name given to the expansive and successful social-welfare legislation introduced by the Johnson administration. The percentage of Americans living below the poverty line dropped from 23 percent to 12 percent.

GREAT MOMENT IN HISTORY

Johnson passed The Elementary and Secondary Education Act, which called for equal access to education and established high standards and accountability. Funding aimed to offer each child fair and equal opportunities.

An apple for the teacher with a twist!

Granola Apples

INGREDIENTS

1 red apple, sliced
1 green apple, sliced
1/4 cup of peanut butter
1/2 cup of granola
1/2 tablespoon of cinnamon
1/2 tablespoon of sugar

DIRECTIONS

Combine cinnamon and sugar in a bowl. Spread peanut butter on all apple slices except for the top pieces. Sprinkle cinnamon/sugar mix and granola on top of peanut butter. Stack slices to recreate apple shape, alternating between green and red slices. Serves 2-4. Tip: Choose two apples that are roughly the same size to make stacking easier.

JIMMY CARTER

39th President (Jan. 20, 1977 – Jan. 20, 1981)
Vice President: Walter Mondale

As a born-and-bred Southerner, Carter loved his corn bread.

Cheesy Corn Muffins

INGREDIENTS

3/4 cup of flour
2 1/2 teaspoons of baking powder
3/4 teaspoon of salt
1 tablespoon of sugar
1/2 cup of yellow cornmeal
1 cup of diced cheddar cheese
1 large egg
3/4 cup of milk
2 tablespoons of melted butter

DIRECTIONS

In a mixing bowl, combine flour, baking powder, salt, sugar and cornmeal. Blend well. Stir in cheese.

In a separate bowl, whisk egg. Add milk and melted butter and whisk to blend. Add this mixture to mixing bowl, and blend well.

Grease a muffin tin, or line with baking cups. Fill each cup about 2/3 of the way. Bake at 400 degrees for 18 to 22 minutes, until muffins begin to brown. Makes 8-10 muffins.

"It is good to realize that if love and peace can prevail on earth, and if we can teach our children to honor nature's gifts, the joys and beauties of the outdoors will be here forever."

Go Green Stir Fry

INGREDIENTS

2 cups of kale, chopped
2 cups of bok choy
1 cup of broccoli florets
1 cup of green onions, chopped
1/2 cup of peas
2 tablespoons of sesame oil
1 clove of garlic
1 teaspoon of grated ginger
1/2 teaspoon of red pepper flakes
2 tablespoons of soy sauce
2 tablespoons of fresh lime juice
1/2 tablespoon of fish sauce

DIRECTIONS

Combine soy sauce, fish sauce and lime juice and set aside.

Heat sesame oil in skillet over medium heat. Add ginger and garlic and cook 1 minute. Add broccoli and red pepper flakes and cook 3 minutes, stirring occasionally so broccoli doesn't burn. Add kale and bok choy, and cook an additional 2 minutes. Add green onion and peas, and cook an additional 2 minutes. Finally, add sauce to pan, and cook 30 seconds just to heat through. Optional: Serve with sesame seeds. Serves 2.

GREAT MOMENT IN HISTORY

On Aug. 4, 1977, Carter signed into law The Department of Energy Organization Act, thus creating the Department of Energy (DOE). The DOE aimed to formulate and implement a comprehensive, long-term national energy strategy.

WILLIAM CLINTON

42nd President (Jan. 20, 1993 – Jan. 20, 2001)
Vice President: Al Gore

"You can put wings on a **pig**, but you don't make it an eagle."

Bacon Candy

INGREDIENTS

6 strips of bacon
2 tablespoons of brown sugar
Crushed red pepper
Paprika

DIRECTIONS

Lay bacon slices flat on parchment paper on baking sheet. Take 1 tablespoon of brown sugar and spread evenly over slices. Rub the brown sugar into the bacon slices so they are coated.

Sprinkle slices with crushed red pepper and paprika. Sprinkle remaining tablespoon of brown sugar on top.

Bake slices at 375 degrees for 25-30 minutes, until bacon slices are crispy, taking care not to burn them.

Remove from oven and drain on paper towel. Let sit for 10 minutes so slices can cool and harden.

GREAT MOMENT IN HISTORY

Under the Clinton administration, more than 22 million new jobs were created, homeownership was the highest in American history, and unemployment was at its lowest in 30 years.

"I've never broken a state law. But when I was in England I experimented with marijuana a time or two, and I didn't like it. I didn't inhale it, and never tried it again."

Brownies

For when you don't want to inhale! Feel free to add your own secret ingredient (wink, wink).

INGREDIENTS

1/2 cup of butter, melted
1 cup of sugar
2 eggs
1 teaspoon of vanilla extract
1/3 cup of unsweetened cocoa powder
1/2 cup of flour
1/4 teaspoon of salt
1/4 teaspoon of baking powder

For the frosting:

3 tablespoons of butter, melted
3 tablespoons of unsweetened cocoa powder
1 tablespoon of honey
1 teaspoon of vanilla extract
1/2 cup of confectioners' sugar

DIRECTIONS

Mix 1/2 cup of melted butter with 1 cup of sugar, 2 eggs and 1 teaspoon of vanilla extract. Blend in 1/3 cup cocoa, 1/2 cup flour, salt and baking powder. Grease an 8x8 baking pan, and pour batter into pan. Bake at 350 degrees for 25 minutes.

While brownies are baking, combine all ingredients for frosting, and stir until smooth. After removing brownies from oven, allow to cool for a few minutes. Then cut, add frosting and serve. Makes about 12 brownies.

Jalapeño Cheeseburger Meatballs

INGREDIENTS
1 1/2 pounds of ground beef
2 jalapeños, finely chopped
1 egg
1 tablespoon of mustard
2 tablespoons of ketchup
1 teaspoon of garlic powder
1 teaspoon of paprika
1/2 cup of bread crumbs

For the topping:
About 30 thin squares of cheddar cheese
30 small pieces of lettuce
10 grape tomatoes, sliced thinly
1 pickle, sliced thinly
30 toothpicks

DIRECTIONS
Combine all ingredients for meatballs in a bowl and mix well. Use your hands to form meat mixture into meatballs. They should be small enough to hold on a toothpick, about 1 inch in diameter. Line the meatballs on a baking sheet covered with parchment paper or non-stick spray. Bake at 400 degrees for 15 minutes. Remove from oven and lay a cheese slice over each meatball. Return to oven and cook just long enough for cheese to melt, about 2-3 minutes.

While meatballs are cooking, prepare the toothpicks. Stack 1 piece of lettuce, 1 pickle slice and 1 tomato slice onto each toothpick. When meatballs are ready, simply spear each one with a prepared toothpick of toppings, and serve. Makes about 30 meatballs.

Bill Clinton loved a good greasy, jalapeño cheeseburger!

GREAT MOMENT IN HISTORY
In 1993, Clinton signed into law the North American Free Trade Agreement, which created a free-trade zone for the United States, Canada and Mexico.

NOT-SO-GREAT MOMENT IN HISTORY
In 1998, Clinton became the second president after Andrew Johnson to be impeached. Clinton was charged with perjury and obstruction of justice after lying about his relationship with intern Monica Lewinsky.

Vegan Butternut Squash Pasta

INGREDIENTS

2 tablespoons of olive oil
1 tablespoon of dried sage
2 pound butternut squash, cut into cubes
1 onion, chopped
2 garlic cloves, chopped
1/8 teaspoon red pepper flakes
2 cups of vegetable broth
Salt and pepper to taste
12 ounces of pasta
1-2 cups of shredded vegan cheese (optional)

DIRECTIONS

Heat oil in skillet over medium heat. Add butternut squash, sage, onion, garlic, red pepper flakes, salt and pepper. Cook about 8 minutes, stirring occasionally, until onion is soft and squash begins to brown. Add vegetable broth. Bring to a boil, and reduce heat. Simmer for 15 minutes.

Remove squash from heat and allow to cool. Transfer to blender and blend well. Return to skillet.

Cook pasta according to directions on package. Reserve 1 cup of pasta water, and add to skillet with squash. Reheat and stir, until water is well-blended. Serve sauce over pasta, topping with cheese. Serves 6.

DID YOU KNOW?

After Clinton left office, he gave up his greasy cheeseburgers for awhile to become vegan and improve his health.

BARACK OBAMA

44th President (Jan. 20, 2009 – Jan. 20, 2017)
Vice President: Joe Biden

"That's one of those where I have to have it taken away. I'll have guacamole coming out of my eyeballs."

Guacamole

INGREDIENTS

3 avocados
1/2 cup of onion, chopped
1 plum tomato, chopped
1 tablespoon of jalapeño, finely chopped
2 tablespoons of fresh cilantro
1 teaspoon of garlic, minced
Juice from 1 lime
Salt and pepper to taste

DIRECTIONS

Peel avocados and remove pits. Mash avocados in large bowl. Add all other ingredients and mix well. Refrigerate at least 1 hour. Serve with tortilla chips. Serves 2-4.

Eat healthy!

GREAT MOMENT IN HISTORY

In 2010, Obama signed and implemented the Affordable Care Act, extending health coverage to approximately 32 million Americans and cutting health care cost. Coordinating with First Lady Michelle Obama, the president also signed the Healthy Hunger-Free Kids Act, which put $4.5 billion into creating healthy school lunches.

Black Bean & Sweet Potato Quinoa Bowls

INGREDIENTS

1 large sweet potato, diced
1 tablespoon of olive oil
1/4 teaspoon of chili powder
1/8 teaspoon of cumin
2 cups of cooked quinoa
1 cup of black beans
1/4 cup of chopped cilantro
Juice of half a lime
Salt and pepper to taste
2 eggs

For the dressing:

1 5-ounce container of plain Greek yogurt
1/2 cup of chopped cilantro
Juice of half a lime

DIRECTIONS

Combine ingredients for dressing and set aside.

Toss diced sweet potato with olive oil, chili powder, cumin and salt. Spread evenly on baking sheet, and roast at 425 degrees for about 15 minutes. Remove from oven and set aside.

In a skillet, combine cooked quinoa, sweet potato and black beans and warm over low heat. Season with salt and pepper to taste.

Spray a separate skillet with non-stick cooking spray. Crack eggs into skillet and pan fry, about 2 minutes. Flip eggs and cook an additional 1 minute. The yolk should remain runny.

Transfer quinoa, bean and sweet potato mixture to two bowls. Top with dressing, and serve an egg on top of each bowl. Optional: Add a dash of hot sauce. Serves 2.

GREAT MOMENTS IN HISTORY

In 2009, Obama passed the American Recovery and Reinvestment Act, which contributed $787 billion to the economy and successfully pulled the United States out of the worst recession since the Great Depression. The unemployment rate was cut from 10 percent to 4.7 percent over six years.

Obama ended the Iraq War, ordering all troops to withdraw from the country. The last military troops left Iraq in December 2011.

Obama officially repealed the military's "Don't Ask, Don't Tell" policy, allowing gays, lesbians and bisexuals to serve openly in the United States Armed Forces.

Red, White & Blue Fruit Salad

INGREDIENTS

1 cup of white wine
1/2 cup of sugar
2 cups of sliced strawberries
2 cups of blue berries
2 pears, diced
10 mint leaves, chopped

DIRECTIONS

In a sauce pan over medium heat, combine wine and sugar. Simmer until sugar is completely dissolved. Transfer to large bowl and chill.

Add fruit and mint leaves to bowl and blend with syrup. Serve immediately. Serves 4-6.

"I see Americans of every party, every background, every faith who believe that we are stronger together: black, white, Latino, Asian, Native American, young, old, gay, straight, men, women, folks with disabilities, all pledging allegiance under the same proud flag to this big, bold country that we love. That's what I see. That's the America I know."

BARACK OBAMA

Made in the USA
Middletown, DE
16 August 2021

46193602R00029